# Refugee Students

# Refugee Students

## What Every ESL Teacher Needs to Know

*By*

**Jeffra Flaitz**

University of Michigan Press
*Ann Arbor*

# ACKNOWLEDGMENTS

It is one thing to know what makes you tick, but another to find ways to express and act on that passion. I am grateful to my friend and mentor, University of Michigan Press ESL Editor Kelly Sippell, for offering opportunities for me to advocate on behalf of immigrant and refugee students through the writing of books such as this one. She has helped give purpose to my life.

# CONTENTS

# Introduction

A drab procession of solemn-faced women moves slowly down a dusty dirt road. Many balance a sleeping or weeping child on their shoulders and a bulging tattered bag on their backs. Is this the image that takes shape in your mind's eye when you hear the word *refugee*? It may or may not be accurate. This is because refugees come from a wide range of economic and social backgrounds and may just as likely to be traveling alone, pulling a wheeled suitcase, and clutching a dead cell phone. Regardless of how we visually conceive of refugees, we tend to recognize the same underlying state that they share—namely the experience of fearful flight amid tragic circumstances, danger, fear, and loss. The semantic web shown in Figure I.1 attempts to capture some of those fundamental elements. What associations would you add?

If you are an English as a Second Language (ESL) teacher, no doubt one of the factors that led you to the field was the opportunity to express and act on your innate compassion. If you are a content teacher, administrator, health clerk, counselor, custodian, or cafeteria worker, you, too, combine your natural fondness for learners of all ages with insight, creativity, resourcefulness, hard work, and practicality. Teachers, in particular, rely heavily on knowledge about learning and learners, which in turn allows them to design effective instruction, to individualize it when necessary and, when possible, to adjust it, and to fine-tune it. All the same, school personnel regardless of their titles can benefit from deepening their understanding of refugee students. Mind you, our focus will not linger on descriptions of the suffering endured by refugees prior to their arrival in our communities. Rather, we will examine some basic truths or **principles** about refugees. Within the discussion of each principle, you will learn (1) **why the information is important to you** as a member of the school community and (2) **what you can do** to help your refugee students now that you are armed with reliable information.

So, faced with the arrival at your school and in your classroom of a distinctly unique group of English language learners, namely refugees, what would you want to know? What essential information would you like to uncover? What questions would you need to ask to avoid the pitfalls of naïvely adopting a one-size-fits-all approach to instruction, interaction, supervision, and management?

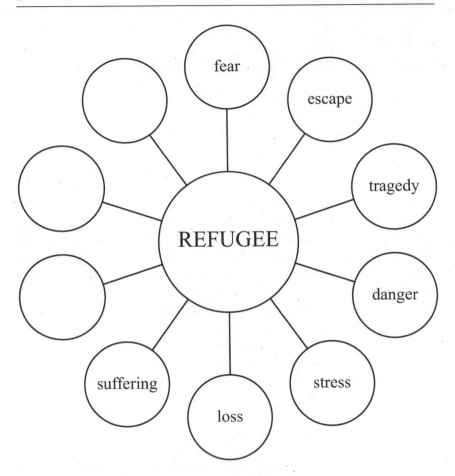

Figure I.1 Some Associations with the Term *"Refugee"*

Begin by acknowledging that your experience and training have already taught you that cultural differences exist among your students and that, individual differences notwithstanding, culture can be expected to affect second language acquisition, classroom behavior, engagement with the subject matter, teacher-student and teacher-parent interaction, and the speed and ease of the adjustment process. Then consider that the refugee experience—though not a cultural phenomenon in the conventional sense of the word because it is not characterized by a common set of values, beliefs, and traditions handed down from one generation to the next—plays an equally powerful role in differentiating ESL students, specifically between refugees and non-refugees.

Your understanding of what makes a refugee student a unique kind of learner is important. It serves you and your students in the same way that athletes benefit from a coach who not only knows the game, the playbook, the field conditions, the opposing team's record, the weather forecast, and so on, but who also knows the unique attributes of each player and what motivates, frustrates, or challenges them, which skills need attention, and how to harness the special intelligence and physical talent of each individual player. In other words, successful coaches equip themselves with information—accurate, abundant, dependable, and specific. Conjecture, hearsay, gossip, and misinformation never won a championship. **By the same token, if we are truly invested in our refugee students' academic and cultural success, there is no merit in accepting misinformation and myths about them when reliably sourced information is so readily available.** The U.S. Department of State, the Migration Policy Institute, the United Nations High Commissioner on Refugees, the American Immigration Council, the Pew Research Center, and many other reputable non-partisan agencies regularly publish highly detailed reports and absolutely readable summaries that can guide teachers and other school personnel to provide effective service to refugee students. These reports can offer reliable insight into where refugees come from, why they have fled their homes, what kind of support they receive along the way, what obstacles they face, what existential options are realistically at their disposal, what assets they bring with them, and what strengths they have developed as a result of their journey. You are encouraged to take advantage of the wealth of current and archived data provided through the websites of these agencies in your journey to become a more empowered participant in the education of refugees. In the meantime, this book will address many of these issues with you—a school-based employee—in mind. We begin with an overview of basic immigrant classifications in case your understanding of what makes refugees unique is a little hazy.

# 1. Principle 1: There Are Many Different Categories of Immigrants.

**What Does This Mean?**

A *refugee* is an *immigrant*, but an immigrant is not necessarily a refugee. So, what about a *migrant*? Is a migrant an immigrant? Can an *asylum-seeker* also be a refugee? Is a refugee an *illegal alien*? Can confidently answer these questions and successfully complete this matching task? (Answers given at the end of the book.)

| | |
|---|---|
| _____ 1. asylum-seeker | a. chooses to leave own country to settle in a new one |
| _____ 2. immigrant | b. flees own country due to well-founded fear of persecution |
| _____ 3. migrant | c. seeks safe haven after having arrived in a new country |
| _____ 4. refugee | d. moves from one region to another within a country to find work |
| _____ 5. illegal alien | e. enters a country without required documentation |

Note: Once asylum-seekers have been granted asylum, they are technically referred to as *asylees*, but for the sake of clarity, we will use the more familiar *asylum-seekers* in this text.

The fact is that, even if the average person may ascribe to most newcomers the same or a similar narrative, U.S. law not only distinguishes one type of foreign-born arrival from another but handles them differently with regard to their legal rights, economic support, and political significance.

## *Immigrants*

Let's begin with the term *immigrant*. While this word tends to be used among the general public as a catchphrase to describe those who leave one country to permanently make their home in another, the U.S. government employs an array of labels to classify different types of immigrants based on their purpose for resettlement (see Table 1.1). In addition, the government distinguishes between *immigrants* and *non-immigrants*. An immigrant visa grants permission to live and work in the U.S. indefinitely as a Lawful Permanent Resident

(LPR). An LPR may apply for naturalization (citizenship) after a specified amount of time has elapsed (usually 3–5 years), though not all LPRs become citizens. Non-immigrant visas, on the other hand, may be issued to individuals whose visit to the U.S. is temporary. Such visitors may include tourists, business people, students, scholars, media professionals, religious workers, athletes, celebrities, and those with specialty occupations in high demand in the U.S., such as nurses.

We might also use the term *immigrant* to denote a person who makes a deliberate decision to leave the homeland permanently in pursuit of opportunities such as reuniting with family or accepting an offer of employment in a new land. That person is said to be motivated by **pull** *factors*. If *immigrant* is the term we apply to one who makes a conscious choice to leave everything behind to establish a new life in a new country, the terms *refugee* and *asylum-seeker* refer to individuals who have no choice but to flee for their lives and are, therefore, motivated by **push** *factors*. With regard to immigrants, bear in mind that not every pull factor qualifies as acceptable grounds for issuance of an immigrant visa, at least as far as the law is concerned. For example, at this moment in time, a foreign national who is inspired by American ideals or attracted by its economic opportunities does not qualify for immigration to the U.S. in the absence of any direct family connection to a U.S. citizen or any type of professional credential. Table 1.1 reveals some of the delimitations on immigration eligibility imposed by the government.

Table 1.1 Eligibility Requirements for Immigrant Visas

| Family-Based | Employment-Based | Special Immigrant | Refugee or Asylum-Seeker | Other |
|---|---|---|---|---|
| Spouse of a U.S. citizen<br><br>Certain family members of a U.S. citizen or permanent resident<br><br>Fiancé(e) of a U.S. citizen<br><br>Adoptee of a U.S. citizen | Person with extraordinary ability in education, sciences, arts, athletics, and business<br><br>Outstanding professor or researcher<br><br>Multinational manager or executive<br><br>Investor | Special Immigrant Juvenile<br><br>Religious workers<br><br>Iraqi or Afghan interpreter/translator<br><br>Iraqi or Afghan who worked for/on behalf of the U.S. government | Person who can demonstrate persecution, or fear of persecution due to race, religion, nationality, political opinion, or membership in a particular social group. | Victim of human trafficking<br><br>Victim of abuse<br><br>Winner of the diversity lottery |

This table, however, does not present all immigrant visa classifications nor does it provide detailed insight into the many restrictions within each category. Suffice it to say that: 1) criteria for eligibility are rigorous, 2) supporting documentation accompanying each application must be substantial and compelling, and 3) processing time can extend to well over 20 years.

Moreover, within each category there is a rank-ordered list of subcategories such that spouses of U.S. citizens have priority over their married children, and married children of U.S. citizens have priority over siblings of the same citizens. As a result, U.S. Citizenship and Immigration Services (USCIS) has had a reputation for being slow to process family-based immigrant visa applications (see Table 1.2).

At the time of the writing of this book, applicants for employment-based immigrant visas fare better as far as wait time is concerned (except for

Table 1.2  Approximate Processing Times for Family-Based Immigrant Visas

|  | All Countries Except | China | India | Mexico | Philippines |
|---|---|---|---|---|---|
| Spouse, minor child, or parent of a U.S. citizen | 1 month | 1 month | 1 month | 1 month | 1 month |
| Spouse or minor child of a permanent resident | 2 years | 2 years | 2 years | 2 years | 2 years |
| Unmarried adult child of a U.S. citizen | 7 years | 7 years | 7 years | 22 years | 13 years |
| Unmarried adult child of a permanent resident | 7 years | 7 years | 7 years | 22 years | 12 years |
| Married adult child of a U.S. citizen | 13 years | 13 years | 13 years | 23 years | 23 years |
| Sibling of an adult U.S. citizen | 14 years | 14 years | 15 years | 21 years | 24 years |

*Data from:* U.S. Department of State (2018d).

unskilled workers). Their paperwork is processed within weeks or months, unless the applicant is from China, India, the Philippines, Mexico, or the Northern Triangle of Central America (El Salvador, Guatemala, Honduras), in which case an applicant who is a researcher or skilled professional may wait anywhere from 4 to 14 years for permission to immigrate. The processing of other types of immigrant visas takes varying amounts of time. It is worth repeating that individuals whose immigrant visa applications are approved do not enter the United States as U.S. citizens, but as LPRs whose status must be renewed every 10 years. LPRs are not required to become citizens. In fact, about 30 percent do not (Gonzalez-Barrera, 2017).

## _Refugees_

Applicants for family-based or employment-based immigration are generally driven by the pull of family or jobs. The decision to leave their homes may be heartbreaking, but they usually have time to pack up their lives, gather the documents they will need, and say goodbye to friends and loved ones. Refugees, on the other hand, are pushed onto the path of immigration due to life-threatening conditions in their homeland, be it war, famine, natural disaster, or political instability. When they flee, their only thought is to escape imminent danger. There is no time to pack, collect birth certificates and school records, or bid farewell to family and friends. Instead, their hasty departure to the nearest safe haven often occurs in the dead of night. Most of the time, there is no real plan, just panic and a sense of urgency. As refugees head for a neighboring country to find shelter, it is not unusual for families to get separated and for individuals to get injured, fall ill, or even die. Stories from the so-called "Lost Boys of Sudan" include accounts of being attacked by lions on their trek from Sudan to Kenya, or captured by rebels and forced into service as child soldiers. Once refugees cross a national border, the host country typically processes the refugees and provides temporary accommodation within a camp, often consisting of tents and housing many thousands of people. The world's largest refugee camp is in Kakuma, Kenya, and holds almost 200,000 refugees. Although some camps are planned communities and have thriving economies, many are woefully underfunded. They may lack clean water, adequate food, law enforcement, basic sanitation, hospitals, or educational facilities. Amid such conditions, refugees languish as days turn to months and months to years. In the meantime, workers from the United Nations High Commissioner for Refugees (UNHCR) interview each refugee to document their circumstances and determine their eligibility for third-country resettlement, if possible and if needed. In the vast majority of cases, refugees in the camps expect to return home when the crisis that plagued their country at the time of their flight subsides. If they are unable to return home, resettlement to a third country can take years and even decades. Only 1 percent of the world's refugees are resettled in a third country (U.S. Department of State, 2018a).

Why do we allow refugees into our country? Our refugee policy is detailed in the Immigration and Nationality Act (INA) of 1980, but the rationale is succinctly summarized in a 2013 U.S. State Department report:

> The United States actively supports efforts to provide protection, assistance, and durable solutions to refugees as these measures fulfill our humanitarian interests and further our foreign policy and national security interests.
>
> (Bureau of Democracy, Human Rights, and Labor, 2014, p. 1).

In other words, the U.S. government recognizes its enlightened self-interest in coming to the aid of human beings who cannot protect or help themselves. As for durable solutions, the U.S. supports:

- voluntary repatriation of refugees when conditions in their home countries permit
- establishment of roots in the host or asylum country until stability in the homeland has been restored
- third-country resettlement for only the most vulnerable refugee populations.

While Congress has not overhauled immigration policy since 1980, they do vote every year on the number of refugees to be admitted to the U.S. The allocation is based on a host of impact analyses, which the President reviews before presenting a recommended ceiling to Congress for their approval (see Figure 1.1).

Contrary to popular opinion, refugee ceilings and admissions remained consistently low over the nearly three decades (1985–2016), relative to peak admissions in the early 1980s (see Figure 1.2). Ironically, the number of refugees across the globe has risen steeply and is currently at an all-time high of 22.5 million people, half of whom are under 18 years of age (United Nations High Commissioner on Refugees, 2018). Some 8 percent of these refugees have no option but to be resettled in the third country. They are

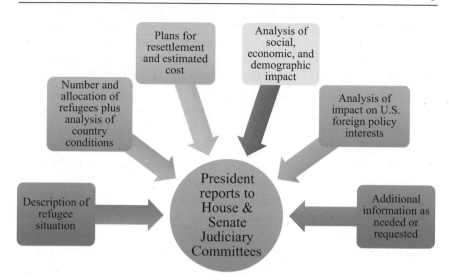

Figure 1.1  Impact Analyses Affecting Annual Refugee Ceilings

given no choice with regard to which country they will be assigned. The remaining 92 percent live under asylum, often in refugee camps in countries close to their country of origin, and wait to return home (USA for UNHCR, 2018). At the time of this writing, the countries hosting the largest number of refugees are Turkey, Pakistan, and Lebanon—all developing nations (UNHCR, 2017).

Of the various categories of immigrants, it is refugees who undergo the most rigorous, prolonged, and redundant vetting process before being approved for resettlement. Refugees must not simply claim that going back home would amount to a death sentence. The burden of proof is on them, **not**

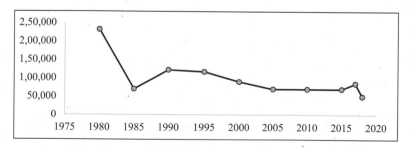

Figure 1.2  Refugee Ceilings, 1980–2018

*Data from:* Migration Policy Institute (2018).

**the agency,** to make their case by producing as much persuasive evidence as possible—not at all an easy task when the best evidence is documentation that is virtually impossible to obtain from their war-torn countries. Refugees are scrutinized and re-scrutinized by multiple agencies before they are determined to be eligible for refugee status, and the vetting process takes a minimum of 1.5 years. Once approved, the wait for resettlement can be years or even decades.

The Office of Refugee Resettlement, working with nine non-profit agencies (mostly faith-based such as Catholic Charities or Lutheran Family Services), assists refugees with satisfying their immediate or short-term needs as they settle into their adopted communities (see Table 1.3). In return, refugees are expected to accept the location of their resettlement unless they already have family elsewhere in the U.S., find employment within six months of arrival and begin repayment of the travel loan (e.g., cost of airfare) within six months of arrival, making monthly payments to help establish credit. The travel loan must be paid in full within 3.5 years.

Table 1.3  Immediate and Short-Term Support for Refugees

| Prior to Resettlement | Upon Arrival |
|---|---|
| • Assistance with travel plans<br>• Travel loan for airfare<br>• English classes (varies) | • Identification of low-cost housing<br>• Airport pickup, transportation to housing<br>• Donations of used furniture and clothing |
| **Limited Time Assistance** | |
| • Cash<br>  • One-time Reception and Placement<br>   Grant ($1850 per person) (for security<br>   deposit, food, clothing, transportation)<br>  • TANF (Temporary Assistant for Needy<br>   Families) for up to five years<br> or<br>  • RCA (Refugee Cash Assistance) for those<br>   not eligible for TANF (amount varies<br>   by size of family and state) for up to<br>   eight months<br>• Food Assistance<br>  • SNAP for low-income individuals | • Medical Assistance<br>  • Medicaid (up to seven years)<br>  • or<br>  • Refugee Medical Assistance (up to eight<br>   months) for those not qualified for<br>   Medicaid<br>• Social Services<br>  • Orientation to community, transporta-<br>   tion<br>  • Job search or job placement<br>  • Vocational training<br>  • English classes<br>  • Enrollment of school-age children |

## Asylum-Seekers

What distinguishes a refugee from an asylum-seeker? Refugees and asylum-seekers are subject to the same push factors that compel them to flee their country and seek refuge in another. However, asylum-seekers cross the border into a safe country before requesting asylum. Many enter legally—with a tourist or student visa, for example—while others arrive without appropriate documentation and subsequently request safe haven. Today's asylum-seekers are less likely to be Cuban ballerinas than Salvadoran victims of gang terror. When Immigration and Customs Enforcement (ICE) officers apprehend border-crossers, they send them to one of the 109 private, for-profit detention centers in the U.S. Asylum-seekers are often separated from their families (even mothers from their young children), segregated by gender, subjected to physical abuse, denied nutritious food and adequate medical attention, and prevented from accepting the legal assistance of scores of volunteer immigration attorneys who regularly descend on the so-called immigration family residence centers. According to the non-profit organization Community Initiatives for Visiting Immigrants in Confinement (CIVIC) (CIVIC, 2018), in 2015 the cost of operating such lock-ups amounted to $2 billion. By law, detention of asylum-seekers may not last more than 30 days. Within that period, detainees have to appear before an immigration judge for a Credible Fear Hearing. Those whose accounts are not considered credible are sent back across the border. If the judge determines that the individual's case meets a certain standard of believability, however, the detainee is to be released within 30 days and given the option of paying bond (up to $20,000), or being fitted with a GPS ankle monitor that must be checked monthly at the ICE office once the asylum-seeker finds a place to live. Although the process just described is enshrined in law, managers of the private detention centers frequently ignore the law and disregard the rights of asylum-seekers. As a result, individuals may remain in detention for months on end, having committed no crime, or worse, they may never be granted a rightful hearing before being summarily escorted back across the border. To reiterate, these practices regularly take place in U.S. detention centers.

Within a year of entering the country, asylum-seekers must officially apply for asylum, which involves convincingly demonstrating in immigration court that they have experienced intolerable suffering and they fear persecution if they return home. Contrary to popular belief, approval of asylum cases is not a foregone conclusion. In 2017, more than 60 percent of all asylum cases were denied (Kowalski, 2017), though outcomes can vary depending on the applicant's country of origin, city where the case is being heard, and the unique disposition (i.e., bias) of the immigration judge. For example, between 2011 and 2016, the denial rate of asylum applications of individuals from Honduras was 80.3 percent while for Chinese applicants the denial rate was only 21.8 percent (Transactional Records Access Clearinghouse (TRAC), 2016b). Some immigration judges grant no more than 5 percent of the asylum cases that they adjudicate; others may approve 60 percent (TRAC, 2016a). Asylum applicants who attempt to represent themselves (i.e., without an attorney) have only a one-in-ten chance of being approved (Kowalski, 2017). All told, pursuing asylum is a tedious, risky, and very expensive process. Moreover, the applicant's life is on hold until the asylum application is approved. Until then, there is no authorization to work or to even look for work, to receive medical or financial assistance from the government, or to take advantage of government-funded English language learning programs.

### Migrant Workers

Refugees and asylum-seekers are not the only group of immigrants who move, or are moved, from one location to another. Migrants (or migrant workers) also travel, but generally from region to region within a given country and for the purpose of finding seasonal work in the agriculture or fishing industries. An individual or family may stay in Florida during the orange harvest, then move to Kentucky to work in the tobacco fields or to Michigan to pick apples, before returning to the South to harvest tomatoes. Being a migrant worker is not synonymous with being undocumented, Hispanic, or a noncitizen. The data in Table 1.4 was collected and published by the National Center for Farmworker Health, which is contracted by the U.S. Department of Labor to annually gather demographic information about the nation's seasonal workers.

### Unauthorized Immigrants

Though a popular expression, the term *illegal alien* is neither a technical nor legal term, and it is clearly not semantically accurate since human beings cannot be legal or illegal. Because legal status is at the heart of the issue, the terms *undocumented immigrant* or *unauthorized immigrant* function more

Table 1.4  Select Demographic Information About Seasonal Workers in the U.S.

| |
|---|
| Estimated number of migrant workers in the U.S..... 2–3 million |
| Percent of foreign-born migrant workers.... 71% |
| Percent of U.S. citizen migrant workers.... 33% |
| Percent of migrant workers from Mexico.... 64% |
| Percent of unauthorized/undocumented migrant workers.... 48% |
| Percent of foreign-born migrant workers with work visas.... 19% |
| Percent of migrant workers residing 20+ years in the U.S..... 31% |
| Percent of migrant workers who speak English at least some English.... 72% |
| Percent of migrant workers who work five to seven days a week.... 93% |
| Average total migrant family income.... $17,500–$19,999 |
| Percent of migrant workers receiving public assistance.... 43% |

*Data from:* National Center for Farmworker Health, Inc. (2016).

effectively as descriptors to refer to people who live in the U.S. without the required authorization or permission to do so.

In January 2016, the U.S. Department of Homeland Security (DHS) (2016) and the Center for Migration Studies (Camarota, 2016) released reports revealing consistent findings about a particular trend in illegal immigration. Both agencies found that the unauthorized immigrant population in the U.S. is increasingly made up of individuals who enter legally and then overstay their visas. In fact, in 2016, visa "overstayers" outnumbered individuals who crossed the border illegally. The DHS refers to the latter group as EWIs—those *Entering without Inspection*. This news announcing the preponderance of visa overstayers came amidst annual reports of steadily declining illegal immigration overall. Despite being reported by the major media outlets, this revelation made little impression on the general public and was virtually ignored by candidates in the 2016 U.S. presidential election. However, it is not too late to discuss with family, friends, colleagues, and even students the findings from non-partisan research institutions about illegal immigration. Consider using this information and that in Figure 1.3 to prompt discussion with colleagues and students:

- Immigrants from non-Hispanic countries such as China, India, and Korea make up 25 percent of the undocumented population in the U.S. (Rosenblum & Ruiz Soto, 2015, p. 5).

| 1,000,000— | | |
|---|---|---|
| 900,000— | successful illegal border crossings (EWIs) | |
| 800,000— | 739,818 | |
| 700,000— | | |
| 600,000— | | |
| 500,000— | | |
| 400,000— | | |
| 300,000— | | |
| 200,000— | visa overstays | |
| 100,000— | 200,000 | |

Figure 1.3  Newly Undocumented Immigrants in 2016

*Data from:* Warren & Kerwin (2017).

- Illegal immigration from Mexico has been in decline for almost a decade and is currently at 1970s levels (Warren & Kerwin, 2017, p. 768).
- Border apprehensions plummeted from 500,000 in 2009 to 193,000 in 2016 (U.S. Border Patrol, 2017).
- Of the approximately 11 million unauthorized immigrants living in the U.S. today, less than 3 percent of them have been convicted of a felony. In the U.S. at large, 6 percent of the population is made up of convicted felons (Passel & Cohn, 2016).
- Every year since 2007, more foreign visitors have remained in the U.S. after their temporary visas expired (thus making them unauthorized immigrants) than have crossed the border illegally. Visa overstayers are estimated to constitute anywhere from 45 to 65 percent of the newly undocumented (Passel & Cohn, 2016).
- The vast majority of undocumented immigrants in the U.S. have lived in this country for more than 10 years. Fewer than 15 percent have arrived in the past five years (Passel & Cohn, 2016).
- Fewer than 5 percent of undocumented immigrants work in agriculture. The majority can be found in service or construction jobs (National Center for Farmworker Health, 2016).
- One-third of undocumented immigrant households include at least one child who is a U.S. citizen (Passel &Cohn, 2016).
- International students are more than twice as likely to overstay their visas than are tourists or business travelers (Ruiz et al., 2017).

• Canadians head the list of foreign visitors who stay in the U.S. after their temporary visas have expired. Also near the top of the list are people from Brazil, Germany, and Italy (Ruiz et al., 2017).

There is no disputing the fact that more than 11 million people are living illegally in the U.S. today, but how good is our grasp of who those people are? As shown, many commonly held assumptions are unsubstantiated. In addition, it's important to take another look at the reasons why people decide to break U.S. immigration law. Pull factors such as economic opportunity and family reunification may motivate some to take the risks associated with illegal entry and residence. Others are driven by push factors that make life back home intolerable—for example, the rise in human trafficking in the Northern Triangle (El Salvador, Honduras, and Guatemala) as well as uninterrupted brutal violence perpetrated by ever more powerful gangs who wreak havoc with virtual impunity. Many in this region see no hope on the horizon and are so terrified for their children that they risk everything to lead them out of danger. For these unauthorized immigrants, the path to legal residence in the U.S. is, for all intents and purposes, an illusion. Marriage to a U.S. citizen is an option, but it guarantees nothing, and the asylum process places a substantial and often unattainable burden of proof on most undocumented immigrants, not to mention a massive financial burden on the family. Nonetheless, there is plenty of evidence demonstrating that unauthorized immigrants build lives here, contribute to their communities, pay their taxes, and adopt a new language and culture over time (See Principle 4, "Refugees are battered but not broken.")

## Why Is This Important?

With a clearer picture of the myriad ways that the word *immigrant* is used for many different types of situations, how does this information affect you as a teacher? First, you are now better informed on a topic that is often controversial. This information can make you a more effective school employee because you will begin to regard all your ESL students with a greater appreciation for how their identities diverge and merge. You will find yourselves naturally paying more attention to their personal lives, not only out of compassion but as a way to gain insight into their actions and demeanor in school. Light bulbs will go on in your head, which will guide you to serve your students with more focus and success. When you hit the wall of frustration over a student's apparent apathy, you may speculate about the source of their reticence from a deeper well of understanding. Is a parent facing the threat of deportation? Is it the anniversary of the tragedy that led to flight from home? Does the presence of the School Resource Officer conjure up associations of brutality and corruption? Does a sudden loud noise trigger a flashback? If a student doesn't realize that the blue color on a world map represents oceans, you might ask yourself if their schooling was interrupted for a sustained period of time rather than concluding that the student is "slow" or ignorant. If a student stops greeting you or participating in class, you might reflect on your own behavior. Did you unintentionally project an attitude of cultural superiority or condescension when you expressed surprise at a student's desire to leave the U.S. and return home to their "third world" country? Maybe making a life in the U.S. was never a choice but a necessity. Also consider the importance of stability in your own life and the feelings of insecurity and fear that arise when too many unknowns invade your universe. The child of migrant workers is often in the dark about how long the stability of this particular school and these particular teachers and these particular friends and this particular home will last. How do **you** respond to the loss of continuity in your life? Do you soldier on, not missing a beat? Do you seek out people who can fill the gaps? Do you plan for the next interruption? Maybe you practice patience, shift into neutral, dream about the future, withdraw, or give up. It depends on the make-up of the individual, but there is no doubt that the absence of control over their course of life is more difficult than usual for the children of seasonal workers.

Caution! To suggest that all refugee students are shell-shocked, all asylum-seekers are disconsolate, all undocumented are paranoid, and all migrants never have a moment's peace of mind is not my intention. After all, individuals bring to the challenges of life a unique set of tools, experiences, and perceptions and may just as easily **not** conform as conform to the expectations of those around them. In fact, if you invite your refugee students to share their stories, you will spend the rest of your career listening to fresh narratives that contain more variety and individuality than imagined. Amid the unique expression of lived experience, you will certainly observe the emergence and coalescence of patterns and themes. Use them, in addition to your insight into each individual, to inform and guide your efforts to connect with and serve your refugee students.

## What Can You Do?

1. **Do:** Conduct a brief interview with each new student. Keep questions generic (country of origin, language spoken, size of family, date of arrival, tell me about your last school, what do you like about school, etc.). Record answers on a bio card.

2. **Do:** Ask students what kind of help they need. You may not be able to follow through with your commitment to keep the different ESL populations in mind as you plan if you are only speculating about how their needs diverge.
   **<u>Do Not:</u>** Ask students about their immigration status. Not only is it against the law, but students may not actually know how the government classifies them. In addition, the question may be regarded as intrusive or embarrassing.

3. **Do:** Educate yourself about refugees and the countries and circumstances from which they come. Search online for "Refugees from X." Look for websites that describe their work as "non-partisan." First-hand refugee accounts are also plentiful on the internet, and numerous books have been published in which refugees tell their stories or authors fictionalize the refugee experience based on authentic accounts. Some recommendations (in reverse order of publication): *City of Thorns* by Ben Rawlence (2017), *Refugee* by Alan Gratz (2017), *Little Bee* by Chris Cleave (2012), *Long Way Gone: Memoirs of a Boy Soldier* by Ishmael Beah (2008), *Say You're One of Them* by Uwem Akpan (2009), *We Wish to Inform You That Tomorrow We Will Be Killed With Our Families: Stories from Rwanda* by Philip Gourevitch (1999).
   **<u>Do Not:</u>** Believe everything you read about refugees. Be circumspect and rely only on unbiased information sources. Once you have deepened your knowledge, **do not** use it to demonstrate how well-informed you are. The purpose of educating yourself is not to impress your students but to build a foundation that will allow you to serve them better. You might use what you have learned to ask questions. Say, "I read that X. Can you tell me more about that?"

4. **Do:** Act as an advocate for refugee students when meeting with and working with other school personnel and help your colleagues understand the unique experience of refugees. Learn how to tactfully address well-worn but false statements about refugees and other English language learners. You could say, "Actually, I used to think

that, too, but then I found this information that said...." Organize a
lunch-and-learn about immigrant categories or immigration myths. If
your school is celebrating Hispanic Heritage Month or International
Education Week, volunteer to extend the traditional focus on food,
clothing, music, and famous people to information about immigration
trends over the years and deeper cultural values. Include activities
such as Two-Truths-and-One-Lie, a fact-or-fiction Kahoot game, or
student-created immigration fact-or-fiction bookmarks.

**Do Not:** Elevate one immigrant group above another, or imply that
one group deserves more attention or understanding than another.

5. **Do:** Reach out to the student's family. Parents may be more willing
and able to share insights about their family's background and
experience. In most traditional societies, teachers are almost as
important as parents in the life of a child. Parents will be thrilled
to receive your attention and will take your advice seriously if you
happen to recommend a certain course of action or type of activity that
will help the student.

**Do Not:** Ignore families or discourage them from seeing you due to a
perceived language barrier. Translation applications for phones are far
from perfect, but they will ensure some level of viable communication.

6. **Do:** Differentiate instruction as best you can. Focus on the most
important concepts. You are not really responsible for teaching
refugees everything they need to know, and students with limited
or interrupted formal education (SLIFE) or lingering psychological
trauma may have difficulty absorbing large quantities of new concepts
anyway. Remember that something is better than nothing.

**Do Not:** Express frustration to students regarding their progress
or your inability to address needs for which you lack sufficient
training. If you teach at the high school level, you may lobby your
state representatives for more lenience with regard to time allotted
to complete high school. You might also persuade administration
to schedule ESL classes in double blocks to allow time for ESL and
content teachers to co-teach, or at least plan lessons that combine
academic language with academic content. If you take positive action,
even if it doesn't succeed immediately, your level of anxiety will drop
and differentiation of instruction won't appear to be as big a headache.

**Do Not:** Assume that all ESL students understand what it means to be a refugee. You may want to plan a unit on immigration. If you find a documentary video that you think might be enlightening and spark some good discussion in class, first allow your refugee students to preview it and give their blessing. If they feel offended or embarrassed by any of the content you bring into the lesson on immigration, they may not share those sentiments with you, so you will want to pay attention to their reaction to the material. If in doubt, jettison the video.

**Do Not:** Focus exclusively on refugees within the topic of immigration, even if your class is 100 percent made up of that group. All students, regardless of their immigration status, should have a basic understanding of this important topic, and they should be given the opportunity to learn from one another, if possible.

# 2. Principle 2: Refugees Are Diverse.

**What Does This Mean?**

Refugees represent a broad spectrum of backgrounds. They are diverse in terms of demographic variables such as nationality, native language, age, gender, religion, level of education, and employment. Their cultural values vary as well, and differences may also be found (even pronounced) across regions within a single country of origin. As in all populations, there is considerable variation from one individual to the next...even within the same family.

Making judgments about people based on their immigration status, country of origin, religion, dress, etc., is widely discouraged, given the well-known tendency for stereotypes to lead to bias, discrimination, and conflict. Consider a practical metaphor: no reputable doctor would attempt a diagnosis without interviewing the patient and reviewing lab results. Nor would a teacher randomly assign a grade without evidence of the student's performance. It's only logical. Therefore, since the best prevention for misjudgment or prejudgment (and the disharmony that it engenders) is factual information, you are now invited to challenge whatever preconceptions you may hold regarding refugees by considering their diversity.

### *Nationality*

Where do refugees who settle in the United States come from? Africa? The Middle East? Actually, the U.S. State Department's Bureau of Population, Refugees, and Migration reports that, from 2008 to 2018, by far the greatest number of refugees came from Asia, specifically from Burma and Bhutan (see Figure 2.1) (U.S. Department of State, 2018b). That number is almost twice the number of refugees who come from Africa and about one-third as many who came from the Near East. In all, refugees from some 111 different countries were admitted to the U.S. during this timeframe (U.S. Department of State, 2018b).

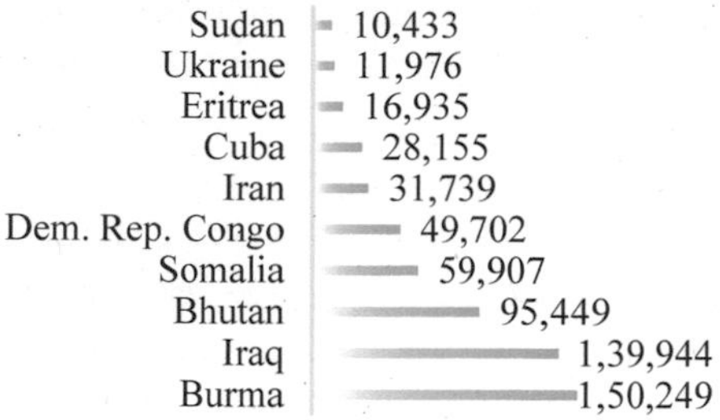

Sudan = 10,433
Ukraine = 11,976
Eritrea = 16,935
Cuba — 28,155
Iran — 31,739
Dem. Rep. Congo —— 49,702
Somalia —— 59,907
Bhutan ——— 95,449
Iraq ——— 1,39,944
Burma ———1,50,249

Figure 2.1 Top 10 Refugee-Sending Countries, 2008–18

*Data from:* U.S. Department of State (2018b).

## Native Language

Because the lion's share of English language learners in U.S. schools are Spanish speakers (77 percent), state legislatures have allocated significant amounts of money to hire Spanish-English bilingual assistants (National Center for Educational Statistics, 2018). Indeed, most of the students who are served by the instructional staff and programs funded by the government are Permanent Residents, U.S. citizens, or unauthorized immigrants—not refugees. Approximately 21,000 refugee children enrolled in U.S. schools in 2016. As shown in Figure 2.2, most of those children do not speak Spanish. Languages spoken by more than 10,000 U.S. refugee arrivals include: Arabic, Armenian, Burmese, Chaldean, Chin, Farsi, Hmong, Karen, Kinyarwanda, Kirundi, Kiswahili, Nepali, Russian, Somali, Spanish, Tigrinya, Turkish,

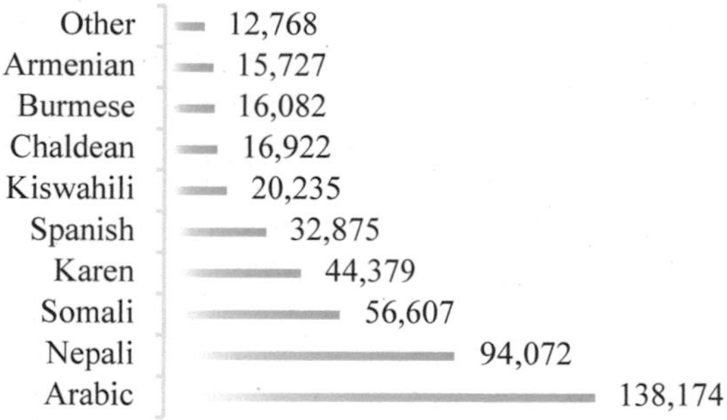

Other = 12,768
Armenian = 15,727
Burmese = 16,082
Chaldean = 16,922
Kiswahili = 20,235
Spanish —— 32,875
Karen —— 44,379
Somali —— 56,607
Nepali ——— 94,072
Arabic ——— 138,174

Figure 2.2 Top 10 Languages Spoken by Refugee Arrivals in 2016

*Data from:* U.S. Department of State (2018c).

Ukrainian, and Vietnamese. This array represents not just an increase in the number of languages spoken in our schools, but a wider gap between and among language families.

Migration flows a century ago (early 1900s) primarily emanated from Europe, and introduced a host of Indo-European languages. Spanish, German, French, Italian, and Russian all belong to this particular language family and, therefore, possess distinctive similarities due to their common origin. Arabic and Chaldean, both spoken in Iraq, belong to the Semitic language family, while Kiswahili (a language spoken in Somalia and Congo), Kirundi (spoken in Burundi), and Kinyarwanda (spoken in the Democratic Republic of Congo) are part of the Afro-Asiatic family of languages. What this means is that we encounter a Tower of Babel as soon as we set foot on campus. The bad news is that our facility with Spanish becomes less useful in such an environment. The good news is that communication, instruction, and learning need not come to a halt. In fact, the more diverse the linguistic climate and the less reliant we are on a common language, the more readily students will and do make the effort to learn English. This phenomenon is known as **negotiation of meaning**. The reader should not conclude, however, that no native language support is necessary as schools guide their learners toward proficiency in English and mastery of the subject matter of the curriculum. Certainly, important school documents, especially those that spell out the school's policies, should be linguistically accessible to newcomers and their parents. The critical issue in the classroom is that the teacher need not be fluent in the student's native language, but should possess some familiarity with basic elements of that language. Does it drop subject pronouns? Does it have a *be* verb? Does it have strict word order? What sounds in English are not used in the language? In other words, teachers need to know which aspects of English will present difficulties, how to locate that information, and how to address those difficulties when planning instruction. In a pinch, teachers and staff can turn to new technology and special smart phone applications to ease communication.

## *Age and Gender*

Many people are surprised to learn that more than half of all refugees that come to U.S. are between the ages of 0 and 24 (U.S. Department of Homeland Security, 2017). Of course, this becomes obvious when you realize that refugees tend to arrive as families headed by a single parent. Lest you be tempted to generalize that the refugee population is young, bear in mind that half

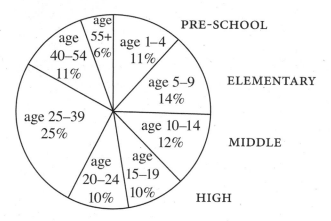

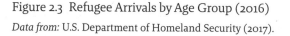

Figure 2.3 Refugee Arrivals by Age Group (2016)

*Data from:* U.S. Department of Homeland Security (2017).

doesn't constitute a majority. In other words, refugees are still diverse with respect to age (see Figure 2.3).

When it comes to gender, be prepared for a little nuance. Consider the fact that worldwide the ratio of females to males is 50/50, but that, in reality, more boys are born per year (worldwide) than girls. However, since women tend to live longer than men, the balance is restored. Does that mean that male and female are equally represented among refugees? The answer is: not exactly. While there is no clear preponderance of one gender over the other among refugee arrivals, the percentage of male refugees can exceed the percentage of female refugees from the same country by as much as five percentage points. What is going on?

When we observe via news and media channels the images of refugees making their way to safety by land and by sea, many of us are struck by how treacherous the journey must be. As a result of this extreme danger, many families choose to spare wives, mothers, and children the trauma of traveling until one member of the family, usually the father, has made the journey ahead of them; later he sends for the remaining family members when circumstances are less risky. The case is not the same for all countries, however. Adult females from some countries might outnumber adult males, as is the case with Syria, where the death toll among men has risen sharply as the country's civil war rages on.

## _Religion_

In our day and time, the debate over immigration reform includes a discussion about limiting legal immigration overall. The ceiling established for the admission of refugees was, in fact, lowered to 50,000 in the first year of the Trump administration, 50 percent fewer than the number President Barack Obama recommended for 2017. The more restrictive attitude toward refugee admissions is frequently defended by those who cite national security concerns, as well as data showing that Muslims made up 50 percent of refugee arrivals in 2016. The aftermath of U.S. involvement in Iraq and Afghanistan, the brutal civil war in Syria, and genocide in Somalia—all predominantly Muslim countries—has created the spike in Muslim refugees admitted to the U.S. In 2003, approximately 8,000 Muslim refugees were resettled in the U.S. compared to almost 40,000 in 2016 (Connor & Krogstad, 2016). However, an examination of religion as a variable of refugee diversity over the period from 2008 to 2018 reveals that Christian arrivals have significantly outnumbered Muslim arrivals (see Figure 2.4).

Regardless of the changes in that ratio, the idea that Muslim refugees pose a national security risk is not supported by the evidence. In 2016, the Cato Institute produced a report called "Terrorism and Immigration: A Risk Analysis" (Nowrasteh, 2016). It concluded that an American faces a 1 in 3.64 billion chance of being killed by a refugee terrorist (p. 4). Nowrasteh

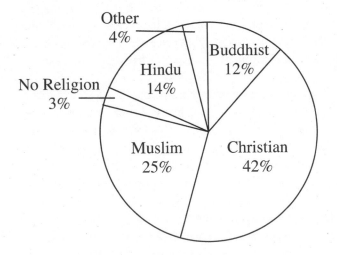

Figure 2.4  Refugee Arrivals by Religion 2008–2018
_Data from:_ U.S. Department of State (2018b).

also estimates that the likelihood of being murdered by a fellow American is 252.9 times greater than losing one's life in a U.S.-based terror attack (2016, p. 4).

## *Education*

Media images of refugees fleeing from danger in their home countries may arouse feelings of sympathy and compassion. The same images may lead those of us on the safer side of the border to assume that most refugees are relatively unskilled and uneducated. After all, wouldn't affluent, well-educated people make their way to safety by car, train, or plane? Wouldn't their clothes and belongings be in better condition? Assumptions of this kind take no account of the loss of even the most basic amenities in a humanitarian crisis. The long, perilous journey takes a toll on farmer and professor alike. As for the role that education plays in the argument that refugees are a diverse population, consider these facts reported by Capps and Fix (2015, p. 3):

- Refugee adults are more likely to have graduated from high school than non-refugee immigrants (75 versus 68 percent). Among adult U.S.-born citizens, the high school graduation rate is 89 percent.
  The percentage of college-educated adults is roughly the same for U.S.-born citizens (29 percent), refugees (28 percent), and non-refugee immigrants (27 percent).
- Of course, these numbers vary according to country of origin as is demonstrated by the data in Table 2.1.

Table 2.1 Adults in the U.S. with a Bachelor's Degree, 2009–13*

| | | | | |
|---|---|---|---|---|
| U.S.-born citizens | 29% | | Vietnamese refugees | 23% |
| All refugees | 28% | | Cuban refugees | 18% |
| Non-refugee immigrants | 28% | | Russian refugees | 63% |
| | | | Iraqi refugees | 28% |
| | | | Burmese refugees | 20% |

*Data from:* Fix et al., (2017).

*Does not include anyone with more than a bachelor's degree or less than a bachelor's degree (e.g., associate's degree).*

## *Employment*

Just as misconceptions about the education levels of refugees are common, so are perceptions about the extent to which they are gainfully employed and living independent of government support. Census data analyzed by the Migration Policy Institute (MPI) revealed that household income among refugees was 84 percent that of U.S.-born citizens, compared with 91 percent for non-refugee immigrants (Fix et al., 2017, p. 18). Among refugees, moreover, there is significant variation, with Vietnamese and Russian refugees exceeding the average household income of their U.S.-born counterparts. Burmese and Iraqi refugees bring in less, 52 and 39 percent, respectively (p. 18).

Employment rates for refugees are actually as high as or higher than the U.S.-born citizen rate, according to Fix and colleagues (2017, p. 16). Approximately 57 percent of U.S.-born citizen adults were employed between 2009 and 2013; the rate was 61 percent for refugees overall and 61 percent for non-refugee immigrants as well. Vietnamese and Russian refugees had the highest employment rate (66 and 62 percent of adults, respectively). Approximately 55 percent of Burmese refugees were employed, compared with 41 percent of Iraqi adult refugees. The MPI researchers maintain that levels of underemployment were also higher among refugees than non-refugees. In other words, refugees were more likely than their U.S.-born peers to have a university degree, but also to work in a low-skill job or have no job at all. Almost 30 percent of refugees are underemployed, compared with 18 percent of the U.S.-born population. When looking at employment according to gender, we learn that refugee men have a higher employment rate than native-born citizens (67 versus 60 percent, respectively); refugee and native-born women share the same employment rate (54 percent) (pp. 15–16).

Despite these data, some people contend that refugees are intent on poaching American jobs and precious American resources. This may be the result of a common fallacy known as the Zero Sum Game (Pelta, 2012). Simply put, Zero Sum Theory is founded on the notion that economic opportunity is like a pie that is not big enough to go around (see Figure 2.5). In other words, resources are believed to be finite rather than expanding, regenerating, or changing. The fallacy (also sometimes referred to as the "scarcity mentality") is that an American citizen loses out on an employment opportunity every time that job is offered to an immigrant. However, as Ana Swanson discusses in her 2015 *Washington Post* blog article titled "The Big Myth about Refugees," research in the U.S. and in Europe demonstrates that just the opposite is the case. She cites the work of Foged and Peri (2015), whose 12-year longitudinal

Figure 2.5  Refugee and Zero Sum Theory: It's Not Pie

study in Denmark found that presence of refugees actually resulted in growth of wages for native Danes and were therefore not an economic burden on Danish communities. Additionally, research conducted by esteemed Johns Hopkins professor Erik Jones shows that countries that place the harshest restrictions on refugee resettlement end up spending more per refugee than those with looser restrictions (Swanson, 2015).

## Why Is This Important?

The ancient Greek philosopher Heraclitus left us with a saying that we all know to be true and obvious: "The only thing constant in life is change." One of the major changes underway worldwide at the moment is human population migration. Because Earth's population is more than 7.5 billion, conflict among us has increased, and the displacement of people from their homes is at an all-time high. As a result, it is virtually impossible to avoid the consequences of living amid diversity. Why should ESL teachers and other members of the school community care about the diversity of the refugee population in the U.S.?

One reason is that resisting the reality of diversity consumes precious time and energy. Our jobs as teachers, while they may not pay as well as Silicon Valley or Wall Street, are perhaps among the most important in the world. Thus, the critical role we have chosen to play in society requires focus. In other words, worrying about the impact of global migration is one thing, but allowing your concern to become a source of conflict once you enter the school grounds is counterproductive.

Once you become more aware of how stereotypes form, you can also prevent yourself and your students and colleagues from falling victim to the fallacies that such misguided myths propagate. As adults, you have the opportunity and responsibility to help learners identify, shut down, and replace stereotypes with more appropriate and accurate profiles. Stereotypes almost always lead to discriminatory behavior.

As you yourself have no doubt discovered, differences between and among people are easier to discern from within than from without. It's just the opposite of not being able to see the forest for the trees. Hasn't something like this happened to you? An acquaintance tells you that you are exactly like your sister, and you protest, "We're nothing alike!" So it is with creating in your mind a profile of refugees or any large cohesive group. Your brain may tell you to identify the totality before turning its attention to the component parts. The lesson here is to avoid judging the proverbial book by its cover. Each refugee is an individual, and unless you exercise some curiosity, you may never discover the extent to which he or she (and others in their group) depart from the one-dimensional biography you have accepted. Muslim refugees are a frequent target of this kind of thinking. In truth, adherence to Islam does not mean that all Muslim husbands wish to have multiple wives, all Muslim women wear a *hijab*, or all Muslim people pray five times a day or ever even visit a mosque—just as not all people identifying as Christian have the same practices or beliefs as others

It is also important to recognize that refugees are proud of their particular heritage. Vietnamese refugees have a historical, cultural, and linguistic background quite distinct from those hailing from Burma, although both could be racially classified as Asian. The same can be said of people from Canada, the U.S., the U.K., and Australia. They would be affronted by the assumption that one group is hardly different from the other group and would likely ascribe to the holder of such assumption nothing short of ignorance. And yet, depending on the context—say, someone from an African nation—there are some similarities other than language (some shared beliefs and practices) common in the Western world.

Finally, understanding how refugees differ along the lines of language, level of education, and occupation allows you to adjust and fine-tune your service as a teacher, administrator, coach, and so forth. Even the knowledge that many young refugees live in households headed by a widowed mother can affect your approach to your job.

## What Can You Do?

1. **Do:** Ask your registrar to run demographic information about the refugees at your school from the past two to five years so that you can get a sense of how diverse the population is. Your school district's English language learner office should have these data as well, and

your state's Department of Education will have information on the broader refugee enrollment in your state. Once you digest the information, share it with colleagues.

**Do Not:** Fall into the trap of homogenizing the refugees at your school if they happen to be largely from the same country or world region. If anything, you now have the opportunity to explore your refugee students' individuality.

2. **Do:** Look up on the internet common errors made by English language learners from a particular language background. The book *Learner English: A Teacher's Guide to Interference and Other Problems* by Michael Swan and Bernard Smith (2001) is an excellent source. It addresses the grammar, pronunciation, and vocabulary challenges that students from more than 20 language backgrounds encounter when learning English. Another is *Keys to Teaching Grammar to English Language Learners: A Practical Handbook, Second Edition* by Keith S. Folse (2016), as well as *Understanding Your International Students: An Educational, Cultural, and Linguistic Guide* edited by Jeffra Flaitz (2003) and *Understanding Your Refugee and Immigrant Students: An Educational, Cultural, and Linguistic Guide* by Jeffra Flaitz (2006). Don't assume that all errors can be predicted on the basis of how two languages differ or are alike. Many other factors influence language learning.

   **Do Not:** Assume that you have to learn the language of your students in order to be a successful teacher or aide. Instead, develop a "cheat sheet" of key classroom expressions in the languages of your students and keep it handy. *Understanding Your Refugee and Immigrant Students: An Educational, Cultural, and Linguistic Guide* (Flaitz, 2006) provides such a list for Amharic, Dinka, Farsi, Hindi, Hmong, Serbo-Croatian, Somali, Spanish, and Ukrainian. So, *fadhiiso* and do your *shaqo guri*. (*Sit down and do your homework* in Somali.)

3. **Do:** Share with your students some examples of refugees who have overcome obstacles and achieved success in the world of politics, science, the arts, etc., and then give them an opportunity to contribute to the collection. Display the pictures and biographies of these accomplished refugees on a board or wall. Help your students visualize a future for themselves where similar successes and achievements might be possible. Make sure that you also share data that demonstrate how well refugees integrate into their new home countries.

**Do Not:** Encourage refugee students to give up on the goal of
graduation from high school. Many school districts have credit
recovery programs that also contain ESL instruction. If the
conventional path to graduation isn't viable, work with your guidance
office to explore options.

**Do Not:** Discourage your refugee students from entertaining
the idea of going to college. Even if their chances are slim, do not
underestimate their drive to conquer adversity, and to demonstrate to
their families and compatriots and to the world that they are strong
and smart.

4. **Do:** Research U.S. immigration history, not just in terms of
demographics, but with regard to policies and public opinion. You will
find that, despite the lofty ideal expressed on the plaque at the foot of
the Statue of Liberty, the U.S. government has a history of passing anti-
immigrant legislation targeting certain nationalities and races (e.g.,
the Chinese Exclusion Act, Cuban Refugee Adjustment Act, the Alien
Contract Labor Law, and various versions defining what it meant to
not be "naturalized"). Nor have the American people been particularly
welcoming of immigrants in general, even from the time of Benjamin
Franklin and Alexander Hamilton. These Founding Fathers supported
restrictions on immigration, with Franklin demonstrating virulently
anti-German sentiments. He wrote of their "swarthy" complexion,
including in that class Spaniards, Italians, French, Russians, and
Swedes. In his 1751 article "Observations Concerning the Increase of
Mankind," Franklin wrote of these so-called "aliens": "Why should
Pennsylvania, founded by the English, become of colony of aliens,
who will shortly be so numerous as to Germanize us instead of our
Anglifying them, and will never adopt our language or customs, any
more than they can acquire our complexion." Perhaps some of our
own ancestors were among those who arrived amid condemnation
and condescension.

**Do Not:** Address past immigration attitudes in class without
anticipating a range of reactions from your students and planning
for how to handle inflamed emotions. Before you proceed, clarify
your objectives in opening up this discussion. Surely, your aim is
not to deepen any schisms that may exist between refugees and
representatives of the host country (which may well include you).
Indeed, this topic may be better introduced to native-born students
or colleagues who can grapple with the implications less self-
consciously.

# 3. Principle 3: Refugee ESL Students Are Different From Other ESL Students.

## What Does This Mean?

Regardless of whether they are refugees or non-refugees, immigrants who must learn English share this same looming, and often intimidating, challenge. If they're newly arrived, they can also relate to one another over the awkwardness of adjusting to a new school, new rules, new teachers, and new friends. Learning how to "do school" in a new country is a process with its own unique aggravations, particularly because the rules of school are often tacit, only to be revealed when one has been violated. Just ask the eighth-grade Cuban boy who was introduced to the registrar and politely kissed her on the cheek! What if, on top of the maddening demands of second language acquisition and school adjustment, your life was made more complex by the consequences of being a survivor?

### Post-Traumatic Stress Disorder (PTSD)

Many refugee children suffer the effects of Post-Traumatic Stress Disorder (PTSD) long after they have found refuge (see Figure 3.1). For some of them, PTSD will follow them into adulthood or perhaps only emerge in adulthood. Non-refugee language learners (ESL students) face difficulties as well and suffer legitimately as a result. The loss of home, friends, family, culture, and country is a monumental event in the life of any immigrant. This is more often the case if that person continues to be a victim of abuse, poverty, isolation, or contempt in his or her home or community. Nonetheless, the nature, cause, and extent of the distress experienced by refugee and non-refugee immigrants may profoundly vary.

### Second Language Acquisition

We have already acknowledged that learning English is a serious enterprise for most ESL students, especially after they enter puberty, and the task is made more complex by their need to acquire social English and academic English

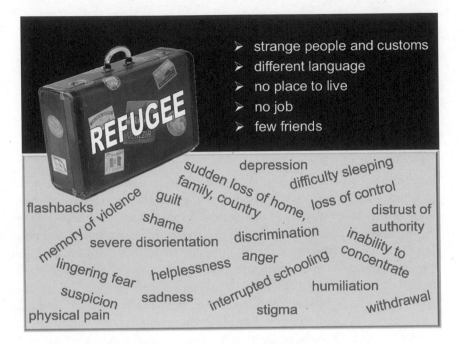

Figure 3.1 PTSD Symptoms Common Among Refugee Language Learners

simultaneously. Yet, school personnel sometimes observe a slower pace of second language acquisition among their refugee students. Let's consider why this might be so. In some cases, refugees may have large gaps in their education prior to arriving in the U.S. During times of war and natural disaster, schools can be damaged or destroyed and rendered unusable. Alternatively, the military may appropriate the buildings to accommodate soldiers and store supplies, including ammunition. In other cases, individuals and families whose homes have been destroyed may take refuge in school buildings. In Syria, one in three schools have been compromised or closed, leaving some 1.75 million school-age children without access to education (Save the Children, 2017). During times of national crisis, school systems also tend to become unstable. Teacher salaries may be suspended and other resources needed to keep schools operational disappear. Consequently, the quality of education declines. Even after migration, conditions in refugee camps or in the refugees' temporary adoptive country may prevent children from going to school. Often families have no means of transportation, or the children are needed to work or babysit while the parents go to their jobs.

How does this affect second language learning? One of the most detrimental effects is the interruption of literacy development in the child's first language, making the transfer of L1 (first language) reading and writing skills to the L2 (second language) that much more difficult once they enter the school system in the host country. Underdeveloped literacy skills, coupled with weak academic learning skills, create a situation in which the ESL instructor and aides must not only teach language and language learning skills but must be patient as the second language acquisition proceeds at a slower pace.

## *Limited or Interrupted Schooling*

Refugee students who have missed out on a significant portion of their schooling are called SLIFE (Students with Limited or Interrupted Formal Education). From the moment they begin classes in their new school, they begin to play a game of catch-up that is stressful for them and for teachers. This is all the more so in the era of high-stakes testing. Consider the student who starts school in Grade 1 in their home country and completes Grade 5. For the next three years, her school is either closed or she has made it safely to refugee camp in another country where there are no educational facilities (see Figure 3.2). Once enrolled in school in the resettlement country, she will be placed in an age-appropriate classroom, which in this case means Grade 9. However, because of the lapse, the student's familiarity and facility with academic content, academic skills, and academic language (in her L1) create a serious deficit that will slow her progress considerably and put her at risk of failing through no fault of her own. The pressure on that student is immense, and her expectation of academic success and will to persevere may waver as she struggles.

Figure 3.2  Example of Interrupted School Sequence

## _Home Life_

And that's just school. Now consider home life. The protracted and exhausting process of adjustment to a foreign environment strains the limits of even the strongest families, but refugee families are frequently destabilized by past trauma. During the transition, adults are also under pressure to meet their families' financial needs while working at low-paying jobs. Getting on one's feet is a struggle when navigating the community means relying on public transportation with its notoriously spotty and slow service. The cost of a car, insurance, gas, and maintenance in the early days of resettlement is a luxury beyond the means of refugees in the initial period of resettlement. Shopping at the special markets that sell food familiar and appetizing to the palate may also involve an expensive and time-consuming trek across town. Sometimes this leaves refugee families to rely on the local grocery store where they attempt to compensate for their preferred dietary choices by purchasing relatively inexpensive and popular food products such as chips, sweets, and sugary caffeinated beverages whose nutritional value may lead to health problems such as diabetes and heart disease, not to mention hyperactivity among children. Additionally, children left at home alone while the parents are at work may be given the responsibility of feeding their younger siblings, and as a result the meals may not be healthy or balanced. Difficulties with transportation and shopping can also disrupt the flow of adjustment, as can limited or non-existent access to computing technology and the internet. Again, the cost is relative. Keep in mind that minimum-wage employment rarely allows for the acquisition of laptops and printers. A family may share a single tablet or smart phone, relying on the local public library for their computing and printing needs.

## Why Is This Important?

Whereas the common condition of all ESL students is the ordeal of learning English, refugees have the additional challenge of coping amid a greater constellation of impediments, and often more serious ones at that. Consequently, they are more vulnerable than non-refugee immigrants and require different attention.

One of the major differences between refugee and non-refugee ESL students, for example, is the more likely possibility that refugees will have experienced some break in their schooling, or no opportunity at all to obtain an education. As a teacher of SLIFE, you may consider yourself to be severely limited in your professional and personal readiness to tackle the needs of this special population. You may begin to wonder if your school district has the resources to bring you and your colleagues up to speed and if you have the time and patience to pursue more in-service training. Actually, students who are clearly lacking the fundamentals of formal schooling are in some ways easier to assist than those whose skills are on the cusp. Their needs are obvious, and teachers tend to plan with those needs in mind. Other SLIFE who don't lag so far behind their mainstream peers may receive less focused attention. You may be misled into ignoring the need to differentiate instruction, or you may use too few elements of sheltered instruction (such as using graphic organizers, simplifying the language of exams, allowing alternative assessments) and offer no role for your students' native languages. It is essential to understand that, despite appearances, refugee and non-refugee ESL students may expend different amounts of time and energy accomplishing the same academic goal and therefore require varying amounts and types of support.

You must bear in mind as well that refugee students experience more pressure to succeed, from within and without, and they are more likely than their non-refugee classmates to drop out of school. They encounter more distractions at home (cooking, cleaning, babysitting, translating for parents, helping parents to acculturate) that prevent them from performing up to their potential. You need to know what their responsibilities are at home so that you can adjust your own expectations. On the other hand, some refugees may be discouraged from achieving in school by their families and instead be expected to get a full-time job and/or marry and start a family. This is especially true of girls from some traditional cultures. When culture gaps are particularly wide, students end up adding the resulting dissonance to their already heavy load. Unlike their peers from places such as Puerto Rico and Mexico, refugee students face greater cultural differences that can impede their learning process. (Culturally, students from Puerto Rico and Mexico share more similarities with mainstream U.S.-born students.) Remember, acculturation is correlated with second language acquisition, and second language acquisition to academic achievement.

## What Can You Do?

1. **Do:** Take advantage of whatever in-service training your school district offers. If you feel overwhelmed and underprepared for working with refugees, your imperative, for your own sanity, is to try to get better equipped.

   **Do Not:** Feel as if your smallest efforts don't add up to much. Refugees have developed certain virtues that support them in times of scare resources (including human resources), so if you fail to "rescue" them, you should not necessarily fear for their future. They will survive. Still, you want them to flourish!

2. **Do:** Make your classroom as safe a place as possible. It should be a welcoming and positive haven. Be mindful of aspects of classroom culture that might cause stress among refugee students with symptoms of PTSD. Fire drills, for example, with their loud alarms and hasty exit of throngs of students and teachers may provoke panic, especially if the exercise has not been explained to the refugees. Loud noises in the hallway or the presence of armed security officers or the principal in the vicinity of the classroom can also stress refugees who associate those things with previous trauma.

   **Do Not:** Press students to participate in class discussion or make presentations before their classmates.

   **Do Not:** Invite a student to come see you after class without first explaining your purpose. Ask yourself if even a general lack of order in class activities or transition from one activity to the next could give refugee students a sense of insecurity and anxiety.

3. **Do:** Understand that second language acquisition among your refugee students may not progress as quickly as that of their non-refugee peers who entered your program, class, or country at the same time. Remember that language learning isn't a linear mechanical process that responds to input alone. It is a complex endeavor that involves the interplay of psychological, social, cultural, cognitive, and physical factors, often under less-than-ideal circumstances. Use what you have learned about your students to expect and accept differences in rate of second language acquisition, but don't stop there. Consider, as researcher Dwight Atkinson suggested in his 2002 *Modern Language Journal* article, that refugee ELLs are like cacti living in a bone-dry desert (pp. 525–526): From day to day, they

survive on the little sustenance Mother Nature offers them. But, when
the rare thunderstorm passes through the desert, their condition is
transformed from survival to an explosion of vitality and color.

**<u>Do Not</u>:** Teach your subject matter without contextualizing it with
real-world meaning and purpose. Part of giving refugee learners the
extra boost they need to accelerate their progress is helping them
make connections with concepts they already know and can relate to.
Given the newness and abundance of academic concepts that often
overwhelm them, refugee students benefit from discovering, with your
help, that they can rely on familiar patterns, examples, and standards
to succeed in school.

# 4. Principle 4: Refugees Are Battered But Not Broken.

## What Does This Mean?

Refugees show us a side of our humanity that we often only discover in ourselves if we have survived a crisis and have begun to rebuild our lives and reflect on the lessons we learned in the process. The hope, courage, resilience, and persistence that can emerge when people are brought to their knees are part of our common human endowment. Refugees personify those noble attributes. The refugee journey itself is a test of the human will, which simultaneously brings out strengths that live deep inside all of us and forces the refugee to grow stronger. Confirmation of the power of adversity as the engine of personal transformation can be found in the writings of any number of venerated philosophers and poets and in the sacred texts of many religions. A few samples are provided:

- "Throw me to the wolves, and I will return leading the pack."(attributed to Seneca)
- "Let me embrace thee, sour adversity, for wise men say it is the wisest course."(William Shakespeare, *Henry VI*)
- "He delivers the afflicted by their affliction and opens their ear by adversity." (*The Bible*, Job 36:15)

Because their battle for survival is harsh and seemingly interminable, there is a tendency to look upon refugees with pity. Certainly, they warrant our compassion, but what about our admiration? By rights, we ought to congratulate them, root for their future success, and spread the word about their courage and determination. If they succeed, we should admire them. If they fail, we ought to sympathize with them.

Sadly, appreciation for the refugees' triumph over adversity tends to diminish as the world debates the economic impact and security issues that their arrival is believed to herald. A discussion of macro-level concerns thus diverts attention away from the personal suffering of human beings caught in a humanitarian crisis not of their own making; it also suppresses the willingness to credit refugees for their strength of will. Until we imagine ourselves in the shoes of refugees, we will likely fail to recognize in them the qualities of perseverance and fortitude that we so admire in friends and strangers alike, who find themselves with their backs against the wall but are hell bent on pushing through hardship and eventually succeeding. However, it turns out that refugees are not a broken mess. Despite the social, economic, psychological, and physical obstacles in their way, there is much data to indicate that refugees demonstrate remarkable resilience.

## *Upward Mobility*

According to their 2017 report, "How Are Refugees Faring?" the Migration Policy Institute (MPI) demonstrates as false the notion that refugees are slow to integrate, do not work, and rely on public assistance (Fix et al., 2017). The data show that refugees rise quickly from dependency. The majority of refugee adults are working within eight months of arriving in the U.S., and they are employed at the same or higher levels as workers born in the U.S. If they work, they pay taxes, thus contributing to the economic well-being of their communities. Employment also enables refugees to get off public assistance. It is true that refugees initially rely on public benefits at a greater rate than do non-refugee immigrants. The MPI report, however, shows that from 2009 to 2011, U.S.-born adults were more likely to be receiving food stamps than were refugees after 10 years of living in the U.S. And while 2 percent of U.S. citizens were receiving cash benefits in the 2009–11 period, only 3 percent of refugees were recipients. The ability of refugees to earn also increases with time. Within five years after resettlement, refugees make 42 percent of a U.S.-born adult's salary, but after 10 to 20 years, their earnings increase to 87 percent of the average U.S. salary (Capps & Fix, 2015, p. 2). Kallick and Mathema (2016) report on the results of the 2014 American Community Survey. It showed that refugees tend to be upwardly mobile in their occupations. For each ethnic group in the study, the percentage of those refugees working white-collar jobs increased by as much as 38 percent after 20 years of living in the U.S. By contrast, the percentage of subjects working in service industry and blue-collar jobs fell over the course of a 20-year span of time (p. 17).

Moreover, refugees in the study compared favorably to their U.S.-born counterparts with respect to business ownership. Roughly 31 out of every 1,000 Bosnian-employed refugees in the study owned businesses—the exact same ratio of established U.S. citizens who own businesses. Compare this with the Burmese subjects who ran their own businesses at a ratio of 26 out of every 1,000 workers. For the Hmong employed refugees, the ratio was 22 out of 1,000, and for Somali refugees in the labor force 15 out of every 1,000 owned businesses (p. 20). As far as home ownership is concerned, we learn that some refugees outperform adults born in the U.S. Some 73 percent of the Burmese refugees in the study and 72 percent of Bosnian subjects had lived in their own homes for 10 years or more, compared with 68 percent of U.S.-born citizen peers (p. 29).

Not all refugees fare as well. The research group tasked with the implementation of a Colorado study called RISE (Refugee Integration Survey and Evaluation) followed a group of refugees, looking particularly at a series of integration indicators that included employment (Colorado Department of Human Services, 2016). In their final report, the authors concluded that unemployment was highest among refugees with health issues, those with disabilities, and those responsible for taking care of children at home. Iraqi immigrants typify this trend. Many have suffered devastating psychological and physical trauma, often while working to support U.S. troops, and are initially unable to work. Among Iraqi refugees are also widows of men who have perished in the fighting. They generally have little to no experience in the world of employment, and they are trapped at home looking after young children as well. Still other Iraqis who arrive as refugees are underemployed; that is to say, an individual may be trained to work in particular professional occupation but is unable to obtain the necessary certification to work in a similar career in the U.S.

### English Language Proficiency

Learning English is another aspect of integration that is a source of difficulty but not defeat for refugees. The existing research regarding the extent to which refugees gain proficiency in English can be misleading, however. Table 4.1 reveals a broad overall picture—namely that refugee immigrants are more likely than non-refugee immigrants to have limited ability in English rather than higher levels of proficiency. These data include new arrivals as well as refugees who have been in the U.S. for a decade or more. They include seniors as well as children, refugees who are not literate in their own languages as well as those with college degrees, those in rural areas as well as those in urban centers where language learning programs may abound, individuals who are surrounded by large numbers of speakers of their home language and those who live in isolation from others, as well as stay-at-home mothers with no transportation and those who are able to take advantage of efficient public transportation. Table 4.1 fails to address improvement in English over time,

Table 4.1 Adults in the U.S. with Limited English Language Proficiency 2009–13

| U.S.-born citizens | 1% | | Vietnamese refugees | 69% |
|---|---|---|---|---|
| All refugees | 61% | | Cuban refugees | 74% |
| Non-refugee immigrants | 51% | | Russian refugees | 44% |
| | | | Iraqi refugees | 63% |
| | | | Burmese refugees | 83% |

*Data from:* Fix et al., (2017).

but data from the American Community Survey 2009–11 indicates that proficiency in English increases as the years pass (Kallick & Mathema, 2016, p. 28).

Many refugee resettlement programs in the U.S. offer English classes at various levels for a limited period of time. Public transportation passes are sometimes provided as long as the learner can demonstrate that they are steadily attending classes.

Availability of instruction aside, ESL teachers know that second language acquisition depends on an assortment of factors, such as age, aptitude, attitude, personality, cognitive style, and facility with learning strategies. Proficiency in English is also strongly correlated with overall adjustment and integration. The Colorado RISE report examined a range of integration indicators including: amount of time spent with representatives of their native culture and with those outside their cultural community, whether or not they celebrated American holidays or attended school events and parent/teacher conferences, whether or not they volunteered at school or in the wider community, the degree to which they felt safe in their community or experienced discrimination, and the decision as to whether or not to become a U.S. citizen (Colorado Department of Human Services, 2016). The study demonstrated that refugees scored higher on the aforementioned integration factors as time went on. Indeed, in Year 4, the researchers found that 76 percent of the refugees in the study fell into the high integration category (p. iii). They also learned that refugees aged 55 or older moved along the integration continuum at a slower pace; nonetheless, they scored in the medium integration range (p. iii). One particularly surprising finding from the study suggested that subjects who fell into the low integration level still played an important role in the attainment of higher levels of integration of family members. By assuming responsibility for cooking, cleaning, and childcare, they allowed other adults to focus on jobs and school and to save money that might otherwise be spent on daycare. Their food stamps provided an additional layer of security for the family. Elderly adults also exerted a stabilizing influence on families simply by serving as a source of life experience and wisdom.

### Citizenship

After the initial goal of finding a safe place to live is satisfied, the majority of refugees set their sights on becoming "Americans" in the literal and idealistically figurative sense of the word. They are eligible to apply for citizenship five years after their status changes from refugee to Lawful Permanent Resident. More refugee than non-refugee immigrants choose the path to naturalization, or the process of becoming a U.S. citizen. Whereas nearly 60 percent of refugees become citizens, fewer than 45 percent of other immigrants are naturalized (Capps & Fix, 2015, p. 3).

### Acculturation

It is important to understand that a refugee's attraction to the U.S. is not material comfort but the abundance of liberties that life here affords. If you're not convinced, try asking a few refugees this question: why did you come to the United States? Their initial response may make reference to jobs, a home, or an education. Drill down, and sooner rather than later you will hear the words *freedom*, *safety*, *law*, and even *happiness*. Yet one of the most popular misconceptions about refugees is that they are drawn to the U.S. exclusively because they believe it will improve their economic power and material comfort. A related claim is that refugees and immigrants in general, "want what we have," and are unapologetic about the economic effect their needs exert on established residents and their communities. Some even believe that refugees arriving from predominantly Muslim countries are motivated by nefarious aims, namely the desire to attack and harm Americans.

While economic vitality may well be a powerful pull factor, it is wise to avoid the assumption that refugees leave their homes to satisfy an appetite for the acquisition of goods and services that typify the American lifestyle. Instead, the pull is more likely to take the form of a range of positive attributes attached to our country, such as increased opportunity in the world of employment, education, and healthcare as well as greater freedom to participate in government and society, to practice one's religion, to express oneself without fear of retribution or discrimination, and to live without constant fear of physical danger. The relative abundance of these assets helps explain why so often the immigrant answers the question "Why did you want to live here?" with "Because I love this country and what it stands for." Even when newcomers do express a desire for a more materially comfortable life, they invariably relate such ambitions to their non-commercial value: for example, "I want to live in the U.S. so that I can buy a house where I can raise my family, welcome my friends, and live in peace and safety."

## Why Is This Important?

Despite the diversity among them, one word that can be used to describe the "average" refugee is *resilient*. We have already speculated that the quality of resilience may emerge from the deep well of human experience locked in our DNA since prehistoric times, and that we all can lay claim to it when the need arises. *Need* is a relative term, though. The demands we face as the fortunate residents of developed nations rarely rise to the level of life or death, and when they do, it is quite rare that entire communities numbering in the tens or hundreds of thousands are affected. Although not every refugee has equal amounts of the celebrated resilience gene, you can count on there being plenty of models of strength among your students. It is important that you invest in this notion because it will motivate you to go the extra mile for these learners at those moments when you are already taxed by the responsibilities of your job. Their resilience might inspire your own. In addition, you can be reassured by the idea that, in whatever ways you may fall short of perfection even as you do your best to help, refugees are tough individuals and crumble-resistant if not crumble-proof.

Another realization that may help bolster your confidence in the value of your work with refugees is that time in country, or length of residence, generally results in improved integration. The role you play in moving your students forward academically converges with the benefits of lived experience in the community. Taken together, instruction and time make for a powerful combination. Do not underestimate the significance of your contribution. As you help refugees build their skill, you elevate the level of their potential earning power and civic participation while simultaneously increasingly the viability of your community. Find out how long your students' families have been in the U.S., and adjust your expectations accordingly.

It helps to know as well that many refugees do not represent the lower end of the socioeconomic continuum. As shown, it is not unusual for refugees to come to this country with professional skills and accomplishments. Even with training and experience, however, securing employment as a professional in the U.S. often requires certification issued and recognized by specific oversight agencies or institutions. Foreign credentials for those in the fields of medicine, engineering, law, and education—to mention just a few—are not accepted or only partially accepted, making it necessary for a refugee to repeat their training or prepare for costly accreditation exams only available in English. Just imagine, if you will, that for some reason you find you must take up residence in China. You have perhaps a decade or two of teaching social studies under your belt, but once you're settled in Shanghai, you find yourself virtually unemployable. Your Chinese language skills are extremely limited, and in order to obtain a position in a local school you must present evidence of your qualifications. The authorities will not accept foreign credentials, though, so they require you to take the upcoming teacher certification exam (in Chinese). In the meantime, you could work in a shop or give private lessons, but your current earning power will not support you in the manner to which you are accustomed for some time to come. Hopefully, this visualization deepens your empathy for refugees in the U.S. who are in a similar predicament. If you learn that your students or their adult family members possess certain professional skills, you may want to explore ways to help them network with peers and find appropriate employment, but there may be benefit to you and your school as well. For instance, skilled professionals can serve as guest presenters in class even if they have to rely on an interpreter. They may serve as tutors for your own children, as consultants for your own personal projects, or as affordable technicians for household electrical, computing, or automotive needs.

## What Can You Do?

1. **Do:** Recognize the courage, tenacity, strength, and patience of your refugee students and praise them for these assets when possible. They are survivors! Give them their due credit. By the same token, show patience when they fall short of your expectations. Be aware of the prerequisites that must be in place in order for them to achieve the goals you have set for them. Ask yourself how well you would perform if the shoe were on the other foot.

**Do Not:** Focus on the past misfortune of your refugee students and fail to stress that their futures are brighter because opportunities for advancement are available. You can also point out that the U.S. is full of examples of refugees who rose to national and international importance. Albert Einstein was a refugee from Nazi Germany and won the Nobel Prize in physics for his groundbreaking Theory of Relativity. Madeline Albright and her family fled Czechoslovakia; she became the first woman to serve as U.S. Secretary of State. Gloria Estefan, a Cuban refugee, won 6 Grammys. George Soros, one of the world's richest people, was a refugee from Hungary. Luol Deng fled a bloody civil war in his home country of Sudan and went on to play professional basketball for the Chicago Bulls and Miami Heat.

2. **Do:** Assign projects that allow your students to celebrate the accomplishments and unique contributions of their homelands—a poster contest, Kahoot quiz, sentence completion task (*My country is* + adjective), values list (What success means to me). Like most of us, refugees grow up proud of the achievements and contributions of their country no matter how modest, delight in their culture and traditions, and cherish their communities.

   **Do Not:** Accept the use of stereotypes or generalizations to describe refugees and their native countries. Never present or allow negative portrayal of a refugee's country from a position of judgment.

3. **Do:** Encourage your students to write a Refugee Students' Bill of Rights. Begin by reviewing the U.S. Bill of Rights for ideas and stress that because individual rights are important in the U.S., they are enshrined in law.

   **Do Not:** Miss the opportunity to point out that the U.S. Constitution protects the rights of "all persons," not just U.S. citizens or permanent residents. Moreover, most refugees are very eager to become "real" Americans, and they believe in the fundamental integrity of the United States despite the struggles they encounter, including discrimination, racism, and anti-immigrant sentiment. Also bear in mind that becoming a U.S. citizen isn't simply a question of desire. Applicants must pass all portions of the naturalization exam (civics, reading, writing, speaking) in English, plus pay $725 in filing fees.

4. **Do:** Review the integration indicators that the RISE project identified as key to refugee success. Then explore ways that you can capitalize on some of those factors. For example, parent attendance at school functions and their participation in teacher conferences can be

increased by offering incentives such as childcare or carpooling. Call on a particularly receptive parent to recruit others.

**Do Not:** Discount the strong bond between the refugee student and their family. More than anything else in the world, the family is the source of the student's identity and sense of security.

# 5. Principle 5: Refugee Students Are At Risk.

## What Does This Mean?

Beware of drawing conclusions from aggregated data about high school graduation rates of refugees and immigrants in the U.S. Such numbers generally conclude that only 61 percent of this population graduates from U.S. high schools, compared with 81 percent of their U.S.-born classmates (Sugarman, 2015). Yet, you have learned in this volume that refugee and non-refugee immigrants are as different as they are alike, such that making comparisons between these two groups about issues as important as school completion is unwise.

### *Inaccessibility to Education*

The fact is that refugee students generally have a far greater mountain to climb as far as education is concerned. Unlike other types of immigrants, refugees have often experienced significant lapses in their schooling due to the dangerous and unstable environments from which they flee and the long period of waiting in camps or countries of asylum to be resettled once their status as bona fide refugees has been established. Consider these statistics concerning refugee education around the world (USA for UNHCR, 2018):

- Five times as many refugee children as non-refugee children are unable to attend school.
- Nearly half of the world's refugee children (3.5 million out of 6.4 million) are not enrolled in school. This statistic breaks down to 1.5 million elementary school children and 2 million middle- and high school-aged children unable to attend school.

• Worldwide, 91 percent of elementary school children and 84 percent of middle- and high school-aged children are enrolled in school. University enrollment worldwide stands at 36 percent, but it's only 1 percent for refugees.
• The ratio of refugee girls to refugee boys who are enrolled school is 8 to 10 at the elementary level and 7 to 10 at the secondary level.

Even as we point out that refugee youth face dramatically different educational challenges compared to their non-refugee peers, it is important to bear in mind that there is also variation among refugees. For example, the amount of time spent out of school pre-resettlement affects graduation outcomes post-resettlement, as does the quality of education in the home country, native language literacy, and age of arrival in the resettlement country. Research by Kallick and Mathema (2016) indicates that among their cohort of Bosnian, Burmese, Hmong, and Somali refugees arriving in the U.S. before the age of 18, graduation rates as high as 90 percent were achieved (p. 22). Their findings also reveal that 45 percent of Burmese males and 49 percent of Burmese females completed university in the U.S. (p. 22). Somali refugees, on the other hand, were less likely to graduate from college regardless of their age of arrival. Some 17 percent of Somali males and 19 percent of Somali females who arrived before the age of 18 received university degrees, compared with 15 percent of males and 7 percent of females who arrived later (p. 23).

These are the success stories. The fact remains that many newly arrived refugees, and those educational personnel who are charged with the task of supporting their academic advancement, face daunting obstacles and lower odds of success. Contributing significantly to this dilemma is the U.S. focus since 1980 on admitting only the most vulnerable refugee populations. This policy and the particular humanitarian crises that have erupted since it was adopted, particularly in Africa and Asia, as well as the steep rise in the number of refugees worldwide, account for the refugee profile that we see today, one in which issues of impoverishment and low literacy loom large.

### _Acquisition of Academic Language and Content_

What specific issues top the list of urgent imperatives with regard to the education of Students with Limited or Interrupted Formal Education (SLIFE)? Clearly, the acquisition of academic English is a priority. It is well known that Cognitive Academic Language Proficiency (CALP) takes years longer to develop than does Basic Interpersonal Communication Skills (BICS) or informal, social discourse. This is one reason why CALP development requires concentrated attention, especially for late-arriving adolescents for whom the graduation clock is running out. Having missed out on significant chunks of schooling, SLIFE (note that SLIFE is a plural term) are also in a race against time to acquire content knowledge, which at the secondary school level is based on previously learned fundamentals and is more complex than subject matter at the elementary level. To complicate matters, SLIFE are placed in grades according to their chronological age, regardless of the amount of education they have received. As a result, an 11-year-old with no formal school experience will still be placed in a Grade 6 classroom. Complicating this situation are high-stakes tests that are used to advance students from one grade to the next and to satisfy requirements for high school graduation. These tests pose additional barriers to educational achievement, eventual employability, and civic participation.

Often unrecognized in this mosaic too is the absence or underdevelopment of academic learning skills. It's important to bear in mind that refugees arrive with a trove of skills and knowledge in other areas—agriculture, for example. Often they are accomplished language learners, having acquired several dialects and languages in their home countries or in the refugee camps. Many are skilled builders, drivers, and mechanics. Your refugee students might have had the opportunity to watch their parents expertly solve problems or serve as mediators, mentors, and leaders. Among today's refugees are tailors, entrepreneurs, computer experts, accountants, teachers, medical specialists, athletes, writers, scientists, engineers, philosophers, and artists. Our schools in the twenty-first century demand that learners master a specific set of academic skills often associated with the higher end of Bloom's (1956–) taxonomy of higher-order thinking skills. The ability to analyze, differentiate, evaluate, generalize, and apply knowledge is necessary and present in the upbringing and schooling (formal and informal) of children in every culture, but what differs is the explicit attention paid to the development of such skills in the context of a U.S. public education. The emphasis on practicing critical-thinking skills in the classroom absent any apparent or immediate real-world purpose may strike refugees as bizarre and discourage them from earnestly performing the classwork that teachers assign.

### The Rules of School

In addition to contending with the considerable linguistic and academic requirements of school, SLIFE also encounter manifestations of school culture that may be foreign and confounding to them, particularly if they have little experience in a school environment. How is a new student to know when it is acceptable to get up and use the restroom? Who tells her that homework that is done with friends the evening before, turned in the next morning, and containing identical answers is considered cheating? How does she figure out how to study for a test, use a scantron, address the teacher, ask for help, work with a cooperative learning team, participate in class discussion, type a homework assignment, research a topic, obtain posterboard, or respond to flirtation, bullying, or inappropriate behavior on the part of her peers?

The rules of "doing school" are normally not made explicit beyond primary school. Much is passed along casually from older siblings to younger siblings or by friends. A student's school chops may also be acquired by dint of uninterrupted exposure over the years of schooling. Refugee students typically find themselves in the dark when it comes to navigating school culture. Without ongoing orientation, they can remain unaware of resources that would otherwise accelerate their transition, not to mention their second language acquisition and overall academic progress.

In the meantime, adjustment to school is often painful. Adults have the advantage over children. Over time, they have usually learned to respond to difficulties with some modicum of grace and insight. Children's journey through the maze of school is replete with opportunities to learn from mistakes, but the process can be demoralizing, especially when one lacks the certainty that "this, too, shall pass." This is especially pronounced among refugee youth who come from backgrounds that have afforded little access to school, or who come from cultures where traditional values prevail and where deviation from those values is discouraged or punished. Refugee students who cannot or will not disguise their lack of ease in their new culture in general and the new school culture in particular are often subject to bullying. They may be ridiculed by their peers for their awkwardness with English, for the contents of their lunchboxes, for seeking out a place to pray during the school day, for wearing a hijab, or for holding hands with a member of the same sex. Worse, they may be told to go back to where they came from. Sometimes they are accused of being terrorists. Without understanding that resources such as guidance counselors are available to help them mitigate adjustment challenges, they keep their problems to themselves and suffer the consequences.

Other solutions, such as creating their own student group, organizing a study buddy system, or advocating for themselves by asking the ESL department to provide cultural adjustment training or materials may never occur to them.

### _Funding for Discretionary Programs_

Nonetheless, important strides have been made by school districts, scholars, teacher preparation programs, and non-government agencies to address the needs of SLIFE, and the efforts of these advocates have resulted in improved educational outcomes, and further down the road, enhanced integration of refugees into the fabric of society. Mind you, such efforts and outcomes are dependent on the financial support of public and private institutions.

However, funding for refugee education, and for education in general, is in decline. Cuts in the national education budget, amounting to billions of dollars, have brought an end to numerous discretionary programs that provide professional development for teachers and after-school remedial or enrichment programs for English language learners. Budget cuts also threaten to dramatically reduce support for refugee students whose schools receive Title I or Title III grant monies. Local and state governments have followed suit, slashing education budgets that affect low-income populations. In addition, we are witnessing the shutdown of refugee resettlement offices and agencies across the country, as a result of huge cutbacks in funding for the International Rescue Committee and other humanitarian organizations (Vongkiatkajorn, 2018). English language training and career development for newly arrived refugees are among the services that these agencies typically offer—another reason why refugee students are at risk.

## Why Is This Important?

In the long run, it is counterproductive to ignore the needs of SLIFE, even if it means the infusion of financial support from the government and the investment of additional hours of training for school personnel. After all, "second-class citizens" are more of a drain on society than are those who can pull their own weight and contribute to the overall well-being of the community. Stressed and frustrated teachers should take some comfort in knowing that their micro-efforts have macro-effects. Once again, however, you are urged to note the diversity that exists among refugee populations—that is, not all refugee students will be SLIFE—so you will approach them differently. SLIFE who arrive in your elementary or middle school classrooms have far better chances of successful integration, regardless of the fact that they have significant gaps in their schooling. Those in high school will require more of your attention, and faith. Keep in mind, nonetheless, that SLIFE are not lacking intelligence or know-how; you will be mistaken if you assume, based on their academic proficiency, that they are not school material and cannot learn. You will witness remarkable progress if you provide your refugee students with the right tools.

You will be compensated as well for the effort you make to help SLIFE learn how to "do school." Many schools now have newcomer kits for students and teachers, as well as orientation programs that address basic but not necessarily obvious norms of school culture. They take a proactive approach to the adjustment process, thereby heading off problems before they become serious.

## What Can You Do?

1. **Do:** Modify objectives as well as materials for these students. If you are a subject area teacher, remember that your primary objective is to increase the student's content knowledge. That is what is tested on high-stakes exams.
   **Do Not:** Ignore the academic language needs of these students. Identify the most important vocabulary in a given lesson and provide an opportunity to practice and review it multiple times. If a particular grammatical structure is used repeatedly in your lesson and it is critical to understanding the content, isolate it and again offer your students the chance to practice it. If you're not a grammar, consult an ESL teacher or *Keys to Teaching Grammar to English Language Learners: A Practical Handbook, Second Edition* (Folse, 2016).

2. **Do:** Teach academic skills explicitly. Provide plenty of simple, real-world examples, and provide multiple opportunities for review and practice. Model them, and discuss their significance.
   **Do Not:** Assume that students with limited formal education already have effective learning-how-to-learn skills. You will need to show them how to approach the tasks you assign. Talk about how to study for a test. Help them organize their backpacks and notebooks. Encourage them to make a study schedule.

3. **Do:** Work with your colleagues to plan and deliver instruction. Team-teaching allows both partners to better understand the nature of subject matter and the linguistic skills needed to process it. Together you will figure out how to concentrate on key concepts and language while maintaining academic rigor.

   <u>**Do Not:**</u> Assume that adolescent students are unable to learn from age-appropriate resources. Offering Dr. Seuss books or any curricula that are designed for children is insensitive because these materials contain unacceptably simplified content as well as simplified language.

4. **Do:** Investigate online resources for students with limited formal education. A clearinghouse known as BRYCS (Bridging Refugee Youth and Children's Services) provides excellent and abundant training modules, videos, webinars, articles, toolkits and other resources specifically designed for refugee students. They also offer Refugee School Impact Grants and publish summary reports once the programs are completed. Also check out the BRYCS Promising Practices Database. *Meeting the Needs of Students with Limited or Formal Education* (DeCapua et al., 2009) provides an overview of the issues, while *Breaking New Ground: Teaching Students with Limited or Interrupted Formal Education in U.S. Secondary Schools* (DeCapua & Marshall, 2011) offers suggestions and resources for teachers.

   <u>**Do Not:**</u> Reinvent the wheel. The influx of SLIFE in our schools has led to the creation of adaptable resources and practical teaching tips.

# CONCLUSION

Being a refugee involves a major self-transformation that can take years, well beyond the time it takes to flee one's homeland. Some say the experience is made up of passage through not one, but three, grueling journeys—escape, asylum, and resettlement. Hopefully, you will never know this first-hand. However, you do have a role to play in the journeys your refugee students traverse, and it may well be pivotal. Just think of the brief rainstorm that transforms the desert into a colorful garden. You will see results from your efforts as well, and you may even find that your investment doesn't come at as great a cost as you initially feared.

The topics presented here were selected with the understanding that, as school personnel, you are accustomed to workshopping your challenges. You are no strangers to committees or to the charge to return with a plan. To boot, you have limited time on your hands so prefer to be presented with a manageable collection of essential information to get you started. With that in mind, the broad and complex matter of immigration as it pertains to refugees in our schools has been pared down to a series of principles—Refugees are diverse; refugees are battered but not broken, etc.—that are based on fact and accompanied by a reminder about why these generalizations are significant in the world of education and offering a host of recommendations to guide you. So equipped, your own journey will hopefully move ahead at a faster and perhaps even smoother pace.

# REFERENCES

Akpan, U. (2009). *Say You're One of Them*.

Atkinson, D. (2002). Toward a sociocognitive approach to second language acquisition. *Modern Language Journal, 86*(4), 525–545.

Beah, I. (2008). *Long Way Gone: Memoirs of a Boy Soldier*.

Bloom, B. S. (Ed.) (1956–). *Taxonomy of educational objectives; the classification of educational goals*. New York: Longmans, Green.

Bureau of Democracy, Human Rights and Labor. (2014). *Overview of U.S. refugee policy: 2013 report on international religious freedom*. Washington, DC: U.S. Department of State.

Camarota, S. (2016). A look at the new Center for Migration Studies' illegal population estimates. Retrieved from https://cis.org/Camarota/Look-New-Center-Migration-Studies-Illegal-Population-Estimates

Capps, R., & Fix, M. (2015). Ten facts about U.S. refugee resettlement. Retrieved from https://www.migrationpolicy.org/research/ten-facts-about-us-refugee-resettlement

Cleave, C. (2012). *Little Bee*.

Community Initiatives for Visiting Immigrants in Confinement (CIVIC). (2018). Immigration detention maps and statistics. Retrieved from http://www.endisolation.org/resources/immigration-detention

Colorado Department of Human Services. (2016). The refugee integration survey and evaluation (RISE) year five: Final report. Retrieved from https://cbsdenver.files.wordpress.com/2016/03/rise-year-5-report-feb-2016.pdf

Connor, P., & Krogstad, J. M. (2016). Key facts about the world's refugees. Retrieved from http://pewresearch.org/fact-tank/2016/10/05

DeCapua, A., & Marshall, H. W. (2011). *Breaking new ground: Teaching students with limited or interrupted formal education in U.S. secondary schools*. Ann Arbor: University of Michigan Press.

DeCapua, A., Smathers, W., & Tang, L. F. (2009). *Meeting the needs of students with limited or interrupted schooling: A guide for educators*. Ann Arbor: University of Michigan Press.

Fix, M., Hooper, K., & Zong, J. (2017). How are refugees faring? Integration at U.S. and state levels. Retrieved from https://www.migrationpolicy.org/research/how-are-refugees-faring-integration-us-and-state-levels

Flaitz, J. (2003). *Understanding your international students: An educational, cultural, and linguistic guide.* Ann Arbor: University of Michigan Press.

Flaitz, J. (2006). *Understanding your refugee and immigrant students: An educational, cultural, and linguistic guide.* Ann Arbor: University of Michigan Press.

Foged, M. F., & Peri, G. (2015). Immigrants' effect on native workers: New analysis on longitudinal data. *American Economic Journal: Applied Economics, 8*(2), 1–34. Retrieved from https://www.aeaweb.org/articles?id=10.1257/app.20150114

Folse, K. (2016). *Keys to teaching grammar to English language learners: A practical handbook* (2nd Ed.). Ann Arbor: University of Michigan Press.

Franklin, B. (1751). Observations concerning the increase of mankind. Retrieved from https://founders.archives.gov/documents/Franklin/01-04-02-0080

Gonzalez-Barrera, A. (2017). Recent trends in naturalization, 1995–2015. Retrieved from http://www.pewhispanic.org/2017/06/29/recent-trends-in-naturalization-1995-2015.

Gourevitch, P. (1999). *We Wish to Inform You That Tomorrow We Will Be Killed With Our Families: Stories from Rwanda.*

Gratz, A. (2017). *Refugee.*

Kallick, D., & Mathema, S. (2016). Refugee integration in the United States. Retrieved from https://www.americanprogress.org/issues/immigration/reports/2016/06/16

Kowalski, D.M. (2017). Asylum representation rates have fallen amid rising denial rates. Retrieved from http://trac.syr.edu/immigration/reports/491

Migration Policy Institute. (2018). U.S. annual refugee resettlement ceilings and number of refugees admitted, 1980–present. Retrieved from https://www.migrationpolicy.org/programs/migration-data-hub

National Center for Educational Statistics. (2018). English language learners in public schools. Retrieved from https://nces.edu.gov/programs/coe/indicator_cgf.asp

National Center for Farmworker Health, Inc. (2016). Farmworkers fact sheet. Retrieved from http://www.ncfh.org.org/fact-sheets-research.html

Nowrasteh, A. (2016). Terrorism and immigration: A risk analysis. Retrieved from https://www.cato.org/publications/policy-analysis/terrorism-immigration-risk-analysis

Passel, J.. & Cohn, D. (2016). Overall numbers of U.S. unauthorized holds steady since 2009. Retrieved from http://www.pewhispanic.org/2016/09/20/over all-number-of-u-s-unauthorized-immigrants-holds-steady-since-2009

Pelta, E. (2012). Immigration and jobs: The dangerous zero sum game fallacy. Retrieved from http://www.thinkimmigration.org/2012/02/08

Rawlence, B. (2017). *City of Thorns.*

Rosenblum, M., & Ruiz Soto, A. (2015). An analysis of unauthorized immigrants in the United States by country and region of birth. Retrieved from https://www.migrationpolicy.org/research/analysis-unauthorized-immigrants-united-states-country-and-region-birth

Ruiz, N., Passel, J., & Cohn, D. (2017). Higher share of students than tourists, business travelers overstayed deadlines to leave U.S. in 2016. Retrieved from http://www.pewresearch.org/fact-tank/2017/06/06/higher-share-of-students-than-tourists-business-travelers-overstayed-deadlines-to-leave-u-s-in-2016

Save the Children. (2017). Syria fighting forces hundreds of schools to close. Retrieved from http://www.savethechildren.org/site/apps/nlnet/content2.aspx?c=8rKLIXMGIpI4E&b=9506655&ct=15005681&notoc=1

Sugarman, J. (2015). Meeting the education needs of rising numbers of newly arrived migrant students in Europe and the United States. Retrieved from https://www.migrationpolicy.org/news/meeting-education-needs-rising-numbers-newly-arrived-migrant-students-europe-and-united-states

Swan, M., & Smith, B. (2001). *Learner English: A teacher's guide to interference and other problems* (2nd Ed.). New York: Cambridge University Press.

Swanson, A. (2015). The big myth about refugees. Washington Post. Retrieved from https://www.washingtonpost.com/news/wonk/wp/2015/09/10

Transactional Records Access Clearinghouse (TRAC). (2016a). Asylum outcome increasingly depends on judge assigned. Retrieved from http://trac.syr.edu/immigration/reports/447

Transactional Records Access Clearinghouse (TRAC). (2016b). Continued rise in asylum denial rates: Impact of representation and nationality. Retrieved from http://trac.syr.edu/immigration/reports/448

United Nations High Commissioner on Refugees. (2017). Which countries host the most refugees? Retrieved from http://www.unhcr.org/news/videos/2017

United Nations High Commissioner on Refugees. (2018). Figures at a glance. Retrieved from http://www.unhcr.org/afr/figures-at-a-glance.html

USA for UNHCR. (2018). Global trends at a glance. Retrieved from https://www.refugees.org/refugee-facts/statistics

U.S. Border Patrol. (2017). Illegal alien apprehensions from Mexico by fiscal year. Retrieved from https://www.cbp.gov/sites/default/files/assets/documents/2017

U.S. Department of Homeland Security. (2016). Entry/exit overstay report, fiscal year 2015. Retrieved from https://www.dhs.gov/sites/default/files/publications/FY%2015%20DHS%20Entry%20and%20Exit%20Overstay%20Report.pdf

U.S. Department of Homeland Security. (2017). Table 15. Refugee arrivals by relationship to principal applicant and sex, age, and marital status: Fiscal year 2016. Retrieved from https://www.dhs.gov/immigration-statistics/yearbook/2016/table15.

U.S. Department of State. (2018a). Refugee admissions. Retrieved from https://www.state.gov/j/prm/ra/

U.S. Department of State (2018b). Refugee arrivals as of March 3, 2018. Retrieved from http://www.wrapsnet.org/admissions-and-arrivals

U.S. Department of State. (2018c). Top ten refugee native languages as of September 30, 2017. Retrieved from http://www.wrapsnet.org/admissions-and-arrivals

U.S. Department of State. (2018d). Visa bulletin for February 2018. Retrieved from https://travel.state.gov/content/travel/en/legal/visa-law0/visa-bulletin/2018/visa-bulletin-for-february-2018.html

Vongkiatkajorn, K. (2018). Trump's anti-refugee campaign just hit a new low. Mother Jones. Retrieved from https://www.motherjones.com/politics/2018/02/trumps-anti-refugee-campaign-just-hit-a-new-low

Warren, R., & Kerwin, D. (2017). The 2,000 mile wall in search of a purpose: Since 2007 visa overstays have outnumbered undocumented border crossers by a half million. Retrieved from http://cmsny.org/publications/jmhs-visa-overstays-border-wall

# ANSWERS TO THE MATCHING TASK IN CHAPTER 1

1:c, 2:a, 3:d, 4:b, 5:e